Platts V Bladon Chancery Proceeding

Helena Ruth Bladon Coney

BladonConey Publishing
Derbyshire
DE65 5FW

https://sites.google.com/site/bladonfamilyhistory/

ISBN: 1519650809
ISBN-13: 978-1519650801

DEDICATION

This book is dedicated to all who were involved in the Chancery Proceedings detailed in this book, with the hope that they eventually found a conclusion they were all happy with

CONTENTS

ACKNOWLEDGMENTS

To all the staff at the various archives over the years who have assisted me.

A special thanks to Susan T Moore, professional historical researcher who has an extensive knowledge of Chancery Proceedings, her book 'Family Feuds' was also a big help

INTRODUCTION

William Barnes was the last of his three unmarried siblings to die, which was days after his elder brother John. William's will and subsequent dispute in chancery proved to be a Genealogical goldmine both in terms of family relationships and descriptions of the people involved.

I had recently knocked down a ffteen year brick wall to discover the baptism of my five x great grandfather in Uttoxeter Staffordshire. With the assistance of wills and information I had amassed over the years, I had proceeded back a further two generations and linked other Bladon trees into mine. From the wills, it was evident that the family were husbandmen and yeoman tenants of the Vernon family of Sudbury Hall. Upon researching the Vernon archive at Derbyshire Record Office, there were deeds and indentures relating to the family in addition to entries in the rental books and manorial documents so it was obvious the family were more than 'ag labs'.

I was first alerted to a possible Chancery Proceeding relating to my family whilst at the National Archives in Kew. I was aware that they could provide a great deal of genealogical information and the catalogue entry *C5/302/23 Bladon v Platts Stafford 1698 Pleading* caught my eye. At the time, I knew an Elizabeth Bladon married John Platts at Sudbury Derbyshire where my family was residing at the time. How she fitted into the family I didn't know as she would have been born during the 'Commonwealth gap'. Upon ordering the document and a copy to study in more detail I realised it was the Bladon's in Sudbury and Somersal Herbert and I needed to find out more! What

I did discover provided relationships, which were otherwise hard to prove in that period, and put my tree back a further two generations.

A search in the National Archives catalogue again under Platts and narrowing the search year proved exciting as there were other papers relating to the same suit concerning the will of William Barnes of Uttoxeter Woodlands Staffordshire. This was duly ordered from Lichfield Record Office in Staffordshire and it soon became clear why John and Elizabeth Platts started a suit in Chancery.

Using books and guides, I discovered that Chancery Proceedings cover five main categories but are all filed in their respective categories at the National Archives at Kew, this and the fact not everything is indexed in the online catalogue makes it even more difficult to find paperwork for each suit.

The Chancery Proceeding categories are:

1. Pleadings: statements made by the parties to a case. These bills, answers, replications and rejoinders are collectively known as Chancery Proceedings

2. Evidence: depositions (sworn examinations of persons chosen by the parties), affidavits (voluntary statements on oath) and exhibits brought into court

3. Decrees and orders: in the course of a suit

4. Chancery Masters' reports: on evidence and subjects remitted for investigation

5. Final decrees – and appeals against them

1 THE BARNES FAMILY

William Barnes the younger was baptised on 5th February 1634 at Uttoxeter Staffordshire, son of William Barnes the elder and Anne Stotwell. He had an elder sister Ellen the younger baptised 8th July 1632 and a younger brother John baptised 1st July 1638. William the elder had two sisters Ellen - the elder who remained a spinster and Elizabeth who married Thomas Bladon on 22nd November 1604 at Somersal Herbert Derbyshire. Thomas was a husbandman renting a messuage and land in nearby Potter Somersal from the Vernon family of Sudbury Hall. Thomas Bladon was born during 1577 at Findern Derbyshire and he and Elizabeth had six children Henry, Mary, William, John, Thomas and Elizabeth. Little did the two families know of the looming family feud that would materialise after the death of William Barnes the younger in 1697, involving descendents of four of Thomas and Elizabeth Bladons children.

William Barnes the elder and his wife Anne resided in Uttoxeter Woodlands, which was an area of scattered houses, one to three miles southeast of Uttoxeter towards Marchington and extending towards the River Dove. From the will of William in 1654, he leaves the *"messuage or tenement with the land belonging which my father in law John Stotwell bequeath unto me called the Woodgate"*. William was a yeoman and, according to the Hearth Tax of 1666 whereby Anne was chargeable to pay the tax, had just one hearth.

Ellen the elder

Ellen, the sister of William Barnes the elder and Elizabeth the wife of Thomas Bladon, was buried on 3rd October 1650 at Uttoxeter. It is thought that Elizabeth Bladon nee Barnes had already died by this time, leaving William the elder the sole survivor of the three siblings. Ellen remained single but she did make a will with an estate worth £101 15s 4d (around £7,000). She states she was of Uttoxeter which indicates she had her own household and didn't live with either of her siblings. She bequeathed all her household and belongings in Uttoxeter to her brother William Barnes and after his death to her kinsman Richard Oldfield son of Richard Oldfield of Uttoxeter Woodlands (Mary Bladon her niece married Richard Oldfield and thus Richard the beneficiary was their son). She left bequests to William Oldfield, Richard's brother and to Edward, William, Mary and Jane Oldfield £20 pounds yearly to be divided between them. Her kinsmen Thomas, William, John and Henry Bladon received £10 apiece. Ellen Barnes the younger her niece and Jane Oldfield (both being her god children) received the rest of her household effects.

William the elder

William the elder died 4 years later and was buried on 4th July 1654 at Uttoxeter in the same grave as his father. His will was proved four months later. He described himself as a yeoman of Uttoxeter Woodlands and left his messuage and land called Woodgate to his wife Anne for the term of her natural life. The parcel of land called the Ladies Moor alias Kitchen Piece, a parcel of land called Pinfold Hurst which adjoined Uttoxeter great moor with the appurtenances (this he purchased off Richard Flyer Esq.) also to his wife Anne. To his eldest son William Barnes and to his heirs forever he bequeaths the messuage or tenement at Woodgate and the land belonging with the appurtenances after the death of Anne Barnes along with Ladies Moor and Pinfold Hurst. The house where William the elder "do now inhabit" went to William along with the land belonging during the terms of the lease. To John Barnes and his heirs forever all that messuage or tenement which Humphrey Biddulph do now inhabit together with all the barns, stables, outhouses, lands, meadows lying and being in Uttoxeter Woodlands purchased lately off Thomas Gilbert. Ladies Moor and Pinfold Hurst (separated from the other land) was also to go to John, this was purchased off Thomas

Middleton. His daughter Ellen received £220, with £20 being formally given to her from her aunt Ellen Barnes the elder. Ellen the elder had also bequeath £10 each to John and William; however William the elder purchased the above land for them with the bequeathed £10. William gave his bed, furniture, long table, and husbandry ware, to William. The poor of Uttoxeter and Uttoxeter Woodlands received 50 shillings.

Ellen the younger

Ellen died aged fifty nine and was buried on 10th November 1691 at Uttoxeter. She also left a will dated 1st November and it appears she lived with her two brothers as she was of Uttoxeter Woodlands. She left to her brother John the land called Georges Park to him and his heirs forever. To William Barnes the younger her other brother she left £15. Elizabeth Fleming, Jane Benbow and Katherine Redfern received all her wearing apparel equally to be divided between them. The total estate was valued at £5 7s which only consisted of wearing apparel as the accompanying inventory shows.

John

John was also fifty nine when he died just days before William the younger. He was buried on 25th November 1697 at Uttoxeter. Like earlier generations of his family, he also made a will, some three years previously when he was finding himself weak in body but of sound and perfect memory. To his brother William the younger he left his real and personal estate, all his houses, buildings, land, tenements and hereditaments lying in Uttoxeter Woodlands and household goods, chattels and cattells, quirt goods, dead goods he paying £5 to William Bladon, son of William Bladon vicar of Hanbury who was the son of his cousin John Bladon. John made William his brother executer; however the will was proved by William Bladon (vicar of Hanbury) and Thomas Butler on 18th May 1698.

Helena Ruth Bladon Coney

2 WILL OF WILIAM BARNES

William Barnes the younger was buried on 29th November 1697 at Uttoxeter, having made his will on 24th November after his brother John had died. The will was proved on 22nd January 1697 at Lichfield. As previously mentioned, he was the last survivor of his family and had inherited a considerable estate.

His will reads as follows:-

In the name of God Amen the four & twentieth day of November the ninth year of the Reign of our sovereign Lord King William the third over England 1697. I William Barnes of Uttoxeter Woodlands in the county of Stafford yeoman being sick & weak in body but of sound and perfect mind and memory (praised be almighty God for the same) do make and ordain this my last will and testament in manner and form following. First & principally I bequeath my soul into the hands of almighty God trusting through the merits of my blessed Lord and Savior Jesus Christ to receive full pardon and remission of all my sins and as for and concerning that temporal estate wherewith it hath pleased almighty God to bless me I give and devise and bequeath the same as followeh. Imprimis I give and devise all that messuage house or tenement & land thereto belonging at Gorsty Hill in Marchington Woodlands with appurtenances now in possession of Robert Redfern to the said Robert Redfern and his heirs forever. Item I give and devise to Thomas Bladon of Somersal Herbert in the county of Derby all that close lying near Bramshall Park called Georges Parks in the possession of George Warner of Bramshall to the said Thomas Bladon for and during the term of his natural life and from and after his decease to be divided amongst the children of the said

7

Thomas Bladon share and share alike. Item I give and devise all those two pieces with a barn standing on and of them called the Croft Hurst in the parish of Uttoxeter in the possession of Edward Hadley to the said Thomas Bladon for and during the term of his natural life and from and after his decease to be divided amongst the children of the said Thomas Bladon share and share alike. Item I give devise and bequeath unto Thomas Butler the younger of Colton in the county of Stafford all my household goods and the swine and geese about the house where I now dwell and all the carts and gears which belong to me except two feather beds in the said house and whereon the servants maids usually lye and the other being in the chamber over the house which I do hereby give and bequeath to Ann and Elizabeth daughters of the said Thomas Bladon betwixt them and except one cart which I do herby give and bequeath unto the said Robert Redfern to the said Thomas Butler and his assigns forever. Item I do herby give and bequeath unto my cozen William Bladon of Hanbury Clerk all the herding and quick stock now belonging to me (except the swine and geese before exempted and mentioned to be bequeathed to the said Thomas Butler). Item I give devise and bequeath all that messuage lands with appurtenances heretofore in two livings but now in possession of George Hunt situate in the parish of Uttoxeter to my said cozen William Bladon and his heirs forever. Item I do hereby give and devise all those two closes called Benjamin Meadow and Marlpitt Ridding situated in Marchington Woodlands with their appurtenances to the said William Bladon and his heirs forever. Item I give and devise to the said William Bladon him and his heirs all that messuagee or tenement and croft in the parish of Uttoxeter aforesaid now in possession of John Morris to the said William Bladon and his heirs paying the sum of 40s yearly to the poor of Uttoxeter Woodlands aforesaid forever. Item I do herby give and bequeath to John Bladon brother to my said cozen William Bladon the sum of five pounds to be paid him within twelve months next after my decease. Item I give and bequeath to Elizabeth wife of Arthur Shurley of Hilton in the county of Derby the sum of five pounds to be paid within twelve months next after my decease. Item I give and bequeath unto Margery wife of Elias Dilks of Hatton in the said county of Derby the sum of five pounds to be paid her within twelve months next after my decease. Item I give and bequeath unto Mary Bottom of Roston in the said county of Derby widow the sum of five pounds to be paid her within twelve months next after my decease. Item I give and bequeath unto Elizabeth wife of John Platts of Potter Somersal in the said county of Derby the sum of five pounds to be paid her within twelve months next after my decease. Item I give and bequeath unto [left blank] now wife of Henry Bladon of the Spath near Uttoxeter the sum of five pounds to be paid her within twelve months next after my decease. Item I give and bequeath unto Rebecca Oldfield of Uttoxeter aforesaid widow the sum of five pounds to be paid her within twelve months next after my decease. Item I give and bequeath unto Edward Oldfield of Uttoxeter Woodlands aforesaid the sum of five pounds to be paid him within twelve months next after my decease. Item I give and bequeath unto John Barnes of Uttoxeter Woodlands aforesaid the sum of five pounds to be paid him within twelve months next after my decease. Item I give and bequeath unto William Barnes brother of the said John Barnes and to Edward Barnes of Newton and to widow Barnes of Newton aforesaid each of them the sum of five pounds apiece to be paid within twelve months next after my decease all which said several legacies of five pounds before mentioned my will and meaning is shall be paid out of the lands and tenements before devised to the said William Bladon and all which said lands and tenements I do herby charge with the payment of them and only them. Item I do herby give and devise all that messuage and tenement wherein I now dwell and those 6 several pieces or parcels of land belonging to whereof and called the Newlands and the other four adjoining to the said messuage wherein I now inhabit as aforesaid to the said Thomas Butler and his heirs forever. Item I do hereby give and devise all that messuage or tenement called the Woodgate house with appurtenances now in possession of Anthony Alkins and John Morris and all those 3 pieces of ground adjoining to Uttoxeter Moor called Lady's moor, Pinfold Hurst and Alias Kitchen Piece to the said Thomas Butler and his heirs forever. Item I do herby give and bequeath unto John, William, Elizabeth and Anne brothers and sisters of the said Thomas Butler the sum of £20 a piece to be paid them within twelve months next after my decease. Item I do hereby give and bequeath unto Thomas Fleeming of Uttoxeter Woodlands aforesaid and George Barkham of the same the sum of ten pounds apiece to be paid them within twelve months next after my decease. All which said legacies last mentioned my will and true meaning is shall be paid out of the said tenements before devised to the said Thomas Butler and all which said lands tenements and hereditaments so as aforesaid to him devised I do herby charge with the payment thereof. Item I will and bequeath that my debts and funeral expenses be first of all paid and satisfied and I do hereby nominate and appoint the said William Bladon and Thomas Butler executors of this my last will and testament desiring them to see the same carefully and honestly performed and I do herby revoke and make void all former and other will and wills by me at any time hereunto made by word of mouth or otherwise whatsoever. In witness where of I have hereunto put my hand and seal the say and year first above written. Item as to the last residue and reminder of my personal estate not herein before otherwise bequeathed I do hereby give the same betwixt my said two executors equally to be divided after my debts and funeral expenses paid and satisfied aforesaid.

Wm Barnes
Signed and sealed by the testator himself and by him published
and declared to be his last will and testament in the presence of
Thomas Webb
William Laythrop
Francis Hunt

An inventory of ye goods cattle and chattels of William Barns late of Uttoxeter Woodlands in ye county of Stafford deceased taken and appraised ye 3rd day of December 1697

Purse and apparel	12	00	00
3 mare & 3 foals & 1 yearling colt	08	10	00
8 cows	18	13	04
6 calfes & 1 heifer at Misty Lane close	05	10	00
one hay rick at Misty Lane close	01	10	00
7 shirks & 2 calfes at Swanfields	11	06	08
hay in ye barn at Swanfields	01	10	00
9 sheep at Swanfields	00	13	04
19 sheep at dreds bottom	03	06	08
hay in the barns at home	07	00	00
goods in the new parlour	04	00	00
goods in ye old parlour	02	13	04
in the buttery	00	05	00
in the little parlour	03	05	00
in the house place	06	13	04
in the little buttery	00	13	04
in the kitchen	02	05	00
in the kitchen chamber	00	10	00
in the chamber over the house	04	00	00
in the cheese chamber	04	06	08
swine and pullen	02	05	00
carts and gears and other material	03	10	00
appary ware and things unseen	04	00	00
in all	**108**	**06**	**08**

From papers filed with the will, the three witnesses to the will were examined at Lichfield the same day the will was proved, as to the signing, sealing and publication of the will and if William Barnes was of perfect mind when he signed, sealed and published his will.

Thomas Webb of Woodford yeoman aged forty and over in his examination stated

That about the time of the date of the will upon which he is now examined this deponent being a near neighbour to the said William Barnes the testator above named was sent for to the said testators house and whilst the deponent was there the said will being written by Mr Lathrop his fellow beings (whom this deponent by going to and fro out of one room into another) saw the said Mr Lathrop with the said testator in the parlour writing the will thereof and nearby him was written in the house place and as soon as was finalised with the name and form it now appears the said testator did first write his name up to the wax dropping at the bottom of the said will and then sealed the same and then published and declared the said will as and for his last will and testament in the presence of this deponent the said Mr Lathorp and Francis Hunt who respectively subscribed their names as witnesses to the signing, sealing and publication of the will in the presence of the said testator who at all and singular was of perfect mind and memory.

Francis Hunt bricklayer of Uttoxeter aged around sixty nine was next examined

That about 2 months ago Mr William Lathorp being sent for to the house of William Barnes the testator alleged took this deponent along with him with him and whilst this deponent was there the said Mr Lathrop after he had been some time with the testator, did write the will upon which this deponent is now examined and soon after he had written it in manor and form it now appear and the said testator did write his name at the bottom of the said will and then did seal and publish the same as and for his last will and testament in the presence of this deponent, Thomas Webb and the said Mr Lathorp who in testamentary of the signing sealing and publication thereof published their names as witnesses to the same as they were in the presence of the said testator who at all and singular as of perfect mind and memory.

William Lathorp of Uttoxeter was the final witness

That on the day of the will upon which this deponent is now examined William Barnes the testator sent for this deponent to make his will which on his said day the deponent went accordingly and finding the testator sick in bed but of perfect mind and memory the said testator declared his mind and will unto this deponent and devised him to put it into form and accordingly this deponent without ? out of the testators himself did present and write what he had declared to him in the said will upon which he is now examined in the format it now appears and after he had read it over plainly to the said testator who liking and understood it very well did first write his name at the bottom of the said will and then sealed and published the same as and for his last will and testament in the presence of this deponent, Thomas Webb and Francis Hunt who in testamentary of the signing and sealing and publication thereof did respectively subscribe their names as witnesses as they respectively appear in the presence of the said testator who was all along of perfect mind and memory

The will along with the inventory was then proved in the Court at Lichfield by William Bladon and Thomas Butler. This was just the start of things to come.

3 LOCATION OF THE ESTATE

The location of the various pieces of land and dwellings are scatted throughout the Uttoxeter area.

Uttoxeter Woodlands is an area at the end of Wood lane where the Uttoxeter golf club is located, south east of the town and adjoining Marchington and Marchington Wodlands.

Gorsty Hill is still a small hamlet in Marchington Woodlands more recently owned by the Bagot family of nearby Blithfield Hall.

Georges Park, in Bramshall Park lies between Bramshall and Kiddlestitch along the northern side of the road from Uttoxeter to Bramshall. There is a Bramshall Park farm along this road.

Croft Hurst in Uttoxeter. No record has been found.

Newlands is just west of Netherland Green in Uttoxeter Woodlands. The tithe map shows a John Wheat renting land in this area.

Woodgate House - the current Woodgate farm was built in 1812, however the club house at Uttoxeter golf club was the farm house of Woodgate farm. This area by the golf course is still known as Woodgate today.

Ladies Moor was possibly in the Town Meadow. The Uttoxeter tithe map lists Ladies Moor (number 924 on the map) as being 18 acres 1 rood and 19 perches of Meadow owned by Thomas Hart Esq. and occupied by Joseph Shipley This is just south of the A50, and east of Derby Road, and west of the River Dove which is still meadow land today.

Kitchen Piece possibly adjoined the Ladies Moor. The Uttoxeter tithe map lists a Kitchen Piece (number 925) as 2 aces 2 roods and 21 perches of pasture again owned by Thomas Hart Esq. and rented by Joseph Shipley.

Pinfold Hurst has no record found but more than likely in the same vicinity as the above two pieces of land.

Benjamin Meadow - No record found but in was in Marchington Woodlands and more than likely in the same vicinity of Marl Pitt Ridding.

Marlpitt Ridding in Marchington Woodlands. The Marchington Woodlands tithe map lists a Marl Ridding Croft used as old pasture of 1 acre 2 roods and 3 perches, a plantation in marl Ridding of 8 perches and Lower Part of Marl Ridding croft again old pasture of 2 acres 2 roods and 8 perches. These were owned and occupied by Robert Blurton and are near Netherland Green and Newlands.

Ditch Botham can't be found but as it is mentioned with the land mentioned below, it is thought it could be the land named on the Marchington tithe map as Barnes Meadow. This was old turf of 5 acres 1 rood and 19 perches adjoining Misty Lane Close.

Misty Lane Close this was arable land of 6 acres, 3 roods and 37 perches in Marchington adjoining what is now Moisty Lane. By the time of the tithe award, Lord Bagot owned the land and it was rented by James Orton.

Upper Swansfield opposite Misty Lane Close was arable land of 7 acres 1 rood and 34 perches again owned and rented by the same people.

Nether Swansfield. The Marchington tithe map shows a Lower Swansfield adjoining upper swansfield arable land of 7 acres 7 roods and 20 perches. Owned by Lord Bagot and rented by James Orton.

William Barnes left the Swansfield and Misty Lane land to William Bladon clerk of Hanbury although it wasn't named specifically in his will. It is interesting to note that in 1694 Mary Browne nee Challoner of Woodford, William Browne her son and Elizabeth Bladon wife of William Bladon Clerk of Hanbury her daughter, sold Misty Lane Meadow, Misty Lane and Nether Misty Lane to Thomas Webb of Woodford Mary's son in law via her first marriage to Walter Jeffery. This being the same Thomas Webb as witness to the will

The map overleaf shows circled in red the possible locations of the land and property.

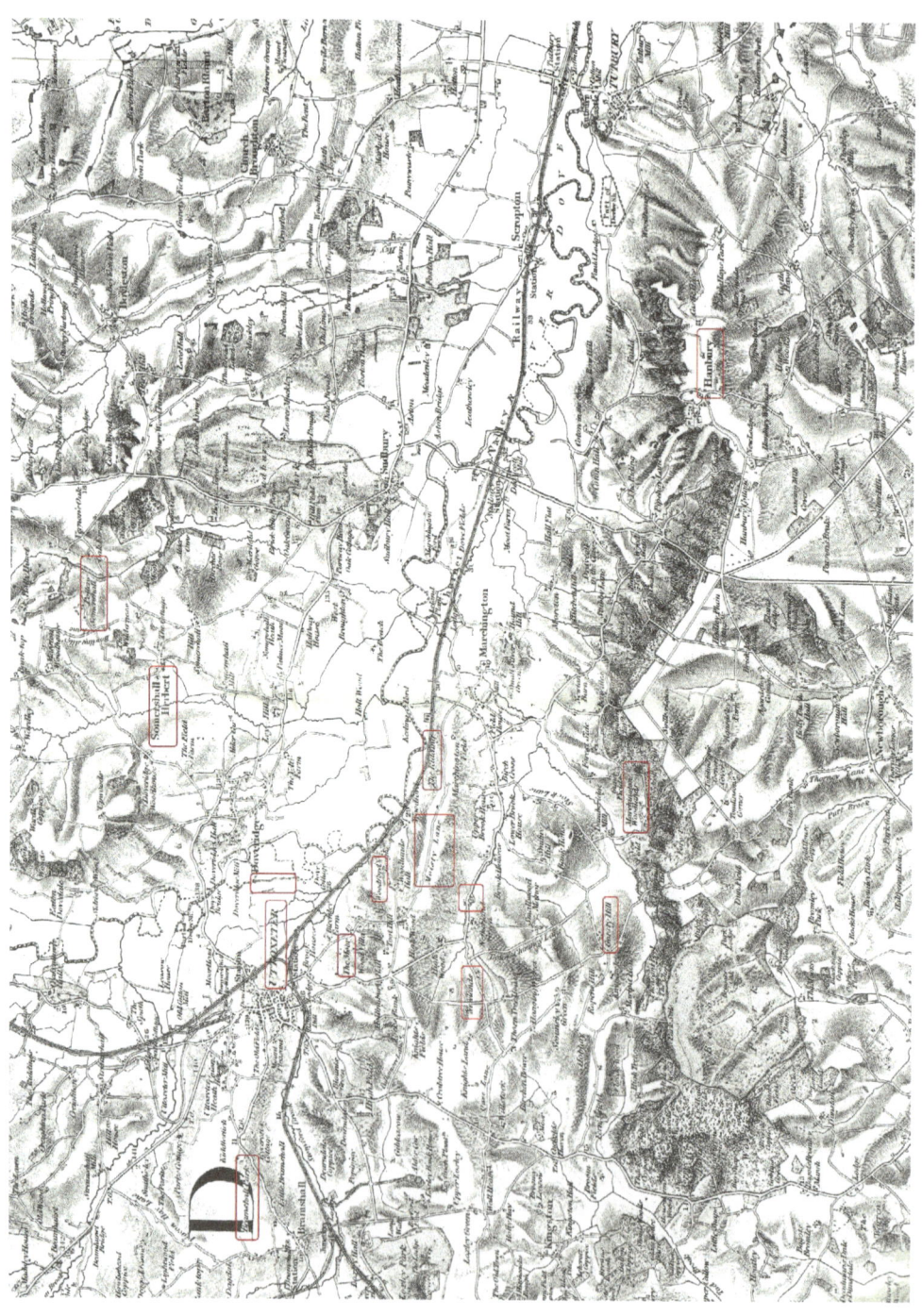

4 MARCHINGTON WOODLANDS SUIT

There were a number of different suits started in the Chancery courts within 5 years of William Barnes death. They all in one way or another involved John and Elizabeth Platts, she being a first cousin once removed of William Barnes. The following are the surviving suits so far discovered at the National Archives in Kew Surrey.

C6/609/71 – 31st May 1698 Bladon V Unknown (Platts?) Collins Division, bill only

The bill of Complaint of William Bladon of Fauld Staffordshire, clerk, against the defendants John and Elizabeth Platts of Potter Somersal Derbyshire. The claim concerns properties left in the will of William Barnes who is said to have died on the 1st or 2nd December 1697 (?). He specifically left property to different people but some of them claimed to be his heirs at law. William Bladon refers to him as his near kinsman. He had copyhold land in the Manor of Marchington Woodlands in the parish of Uttoxeter, called Ditch Botham, Misty Lane Close, Upper Swansfield and Nether Swansfield (occupied by George Hunt and worth £12 a year) which he intended to leave to William Bladon but as copyhold could not be left by will but had to be entered at the Manor Court, and the Court Steward was away as Barnes was dying, he wrote a letter of attorney witnessed by four other copyholders and this enabled William Bladon to enter into possession after William Barnes's death. Then Elizabeth daughter of Henry Bladon who had married John Platts husbandman of Potter

Somersal Derbyshire claimed to be William Barnes heir at law and William Bladon agreed to pay her £100 in exchange for letting him keep the copyholds. He claimed to have given her the money but she had still entered herself as heir at law at the Manor Court and actually moved her cattle onto the fields.

William Bladon and Thomas Butler the younger of Colton Staffordshire yeoman were the executors of William Barnes' will but Thomas Butler insisted on keeping the original copy so William Bladon was demanding that he produce it at the Chancery court. Thomas Butler was one of the alleged confederates; the others were Robert Redfern of Marchington Woodlands, Thomas Bladon husbandman of Somersal Herbert Derbyshire and Henry Barnes of Uttoxeter whittawer (who also claimed to be a heir at law of William Barnes). Another property mentioned was Benjamin Meadow and Marlepitt Riddings in Marchington Woodlands occupied by John Morris which was charged in William Barnes' will with 40 shillings per year to the poor of Marchington Woodlands forever.

C5/302/23 – 1698 Stafford Bladon V Platts Bridges Division answer only

The answers of John and Elizabeth Platts (the defendants) to the complaint (C6/609/71) of William Bladon of Fauld Staffordshire.

The joint answers of John and Elizabeth Platts, the two defendants to the bill of complaint of William Bladon clerk. They believe they are strangers to the greatest part of the estate of William Barnes in the will named but nothing yet appearing to the contrary, that he was seized of the freehold and copyhold lands in the bill named by claims there is a letter of Attorney to the Lord of the manor. Elizabeth is heir at law to William Barnes, being daughter and heir of Henry Bladon eldest son of Thomas and Elizabeth his wife who was sister of William Barnes the testator's father. John Platts having had suspicions that Elizabeth his wife was heir he did attend the Manor Court after the death of William Barnes to oppose the admittance of William Bladon but the steward there did not admit him which John Platts thought (being ignorant of law) to be some sort of judgment and determination against him. It was however to determine whether

Elizabeth was heir at law to William Barnes and to determine the relationship between William Barnes and Elizabeth Platts. John Platts knew which registers to search and the position of the other branches. William Bladon had a letter from his attorney which he thought should be sufficient in law to make him a good title to land. To settle the dispute, William Bladon offered half the value of the land - £100 for their eight and the charges of the fine. After John Platts sealed the articles, William Bladon informed him Elizabeth Plats was heir at law to the copy hold land and he then sealed a bond of the law date and writing to the agreement between William Bladon and John Platts. John Platts then found out the land was worth £16 or £17 pounds a year or £200-£220. Elizabeth Platts did not know anything about the articles of agreement and bond or was privy to the same until three or four days after she got home to Potter Somersal before any agreement was entered to and John Platts told her that sealed articles of agreement but she was heir at law. They also deny impounding William Bladons cattle.

Marchington Manor Court Rolls

The only other paper work found for this case was in the Marchington Manor Court rolls for 1699 held at Staffordshire Record Office.

The first is the admission of Elizabeth Platts to the tenancy, after the death of William Barnes

At this court it was ascertained by the aforesaid Homage that William Barnes, who held of the lord of this manor for himself and his heirs, by copy of court roll of the aforesaid manor, according to the custom of the same manor, all that close or parcel of land called Ditch. Botham Misty Lane Close, Upper Swansfield and Nether Swansfield with appurtenances lying and being within the manor of Marchington aforesaid, had died since the last court, as a result of which there fell due to the lord of the aforesaid manor the best beast of that William as a heriot. And that Elizabeth Plats, wife of John Plats, is kin and nearest heir of the aforesaid William and is of full age. And to this same Court the aforesaid Elizabeth Plats came in her own proper person and sought to be admitted tenant to the premises, to whom the lord, through his steward, then granted seisin by the rod, (for her) to have for herself and her heirs forever, to hold of the lord by the rod, at the will of the lord, according to the custom of the aforesaid manor, for the rent and service thence formerly due and by right. And she was thence admitted tenant.

The second is titled Bladon from Platts and his wife

To this court came John Platts and Elizabeth his wife in their own proper persons (that same Elizabeth was examined by the aforesaid steward, alone and separately, in the absence of her husband, and made surrender freely and of her own spontaneous will and by her own agreement) and surrendered into the hands of the lord of the manor aforesaid by the rod, according to the custom of the same manor, All that close or parcel of land called Ditch Botham Misty Lane Close Upper Swansfield and Neather Swansfield with appurtenances lying and being in the manor of Marchington aforesaid To the benefit and use of William Bladon, clerk, for and during the term of his natural life. And from and after his death then to the benefit and use and purposes that he the aforesaid William Bladon by his last will and testament or by sealed documents in writing, in the presence of three or more credible witnesses, shall determine, limit and appoint; and for the lack of such limitation or appointment, then for the benefit and use of the heirs of the aforesaid William Bladon forever. And to the same Court came the aforesaid William Bladon in his own proper person and sought to be admitted tenant of the premises, to whom the lord, through his aforesaid steward, then granted seisin by the rod, to have as aforesaid (and) to hold of the lord by the rod, to the will of the lord, according to the custom of the aforesaid manor, for the rent and service thence formerly due and by right accustomed. And he gave to the lord of the manor aforesaid as a fine for entry ten pounds, and did fealty to the lord. And he was thence admitted tenant.

On 15th May 1699 in the Court rolls is a payment from William Bladon of £26, consisting of a £10 fine from William Bladon and £16 from Platts – William Bladon paying the entire fine. This appears to be the fine mentioned above.

Exactly two years later on 5th May 1701 William Bladon surrendered Ditch Botham, Upper Swansfield and Nether Swansfield

The view of the frankpledge of the Lord Baron the honorable Charles Egerton of the aforesaid manor held at Marchington within the aforesaid manor on the fifth day of May in the thirteenth year of our Lord William iii by the grace of God of England Scotland France and Ireland king defender of the faith and in the year of our Lord 1701 before Hugh Bateman steward of the aforesaid manor. To this court comes William Bladon clerk in his own person and renders back into the hands of the lord of the aforesaid manor virgate by custom of the same manor all that close or parcel of land called Ditch Botham Upper Swansfield and Nether Swansfield with appurtenances lately or recently in the tenure of occupation of Luke Devill and John Woolley or their assigns lying and being within the Manor of Marchington aforesaid to the service and use of John Moreton junior for and during the term of his natural life and after his death then to those prearranged services uses and interests which the aforesaid John Moreton through testament by his will or through deed or deeds lawfully made in writing by him himself shall limit and appoint and for the deceased thence held to service and use are the rightful heirs of the aforesaid John Moreton forever and to the same court comes the aforesaid John Moreton in his own person and seeks to be admitted as tenant of the said premises and yielded to the aforesaid Lord through the aforesaid steward seisin through virgate in the aforesaid form tenant of the Lord by virgate willingly by custom of the same manor he renders and serves thence before he owes and from right custom gives the Lord of the manor aforesaid through fine of £11 and 10 shillings to the lord faithfully and is admitted as tenant.

John Morton now admitted and fine paid but 8s. paid for f...(?)

William Bladon also appears to have sold Misty Lane Close to Thomas Webb as when Thomas died in 1708 he states in his will

I doe hereby give devise and bequeath unto my daughter Elizabeth Webb and to her Heirs and Assigns for ever All those two Closes called by the names of the Swans fields that I lately purchased of

William Porter of Marchington paying fifty shillings yearly for Ever In bre(a)d unto the poor of Marchington and Marchington Woodlands And allsoe one Close more that I lately purchased of and from Mr. William Bladon of Hanbury Clarke called by the name of the nether misty lane Close or by what other name or names the same is called or knowne.

So from the above evidence it appears that William Barnes's wishes were upheld and William Bladon received the copyhold land in Marchington Manor which he later sold to John Moreton and Thomas Webb. The above case was the only suit brought to Chancery not by the Platts i.e. they were the defendants.

5 GEORGES PARK AND CROFT HURST SUIT

C6/460/11 – 26 July 1700 Platts V Bladen Collins Division, bill, answer and schedule

John Platts of Potter Somersal yeoman and Elizabeth his wife cousin and heir of William Barnes late of Uttoxeter Woodlands yeoman deceased. He was seized in his demise of Georges Park in Bromshall Park, in procession of George Warner, and two closes called Croft Hurst in the procession of Edward Hadley on or about the four and twentieth day of November 1697. William Barnes made his last will and testament in writing and assigned the said land to Thomas Bladon of Somersal Herbert for and during the term of his natural life and after to be divided amongst his children. About the five and twentieth day of March 1698 Thomas Bladon died leaving issue Anne, Elizabeth, William, John, Thomas and Mary all infants under 21 and received the said land. Rent continued to be paid by Hadley and Warner to Anne widow of the said Thomas. About the seventh day of November 1698 Anne daughter of Thomas died. One sixth part of the premises to be divided to the heir at law Elizabeth Platts the sole daughter and heir of Henry Bladon the son and heir of Thomas Bladon of Potter Somersal and Elizabeth his wife both deceased, Elizabeth was sister of the whole blood of William Barnes, father of the said William Barnes. The said William Barnes father had neither brother nor any sister besides Elizabeth and Ellen who died unmarried without issue. William Barnes the son had one brother John and sister Ellen both died unmarried and without issue

30th October 1700 – The children of Thomas Bladon fit to answer the bill of complaint and appoint their mother Anne guardian

The answers of Anne Bladon widow and Elizabeth, William, John, Thomas and Mary Bladon and also George Warner and Edward Hadley. They state that William Barnes did make his last will and testament and appointed Thomas Bladon the land in question for his life and after to be divided between the children of Thomas share and share alike. They are advised that it appears by the words of the will that William Barnes intent was to dispose of all his estate and that the words in the will? with another part are insufficient to cost the inheritance of the said land in the children of Thomas Bladon. William Barnes died soon after making his will and Thomas Bladon entered and enjoyed the said premises for the term of his natural life and since his daughter Anne has died. That upon her death any part of the premises did convert to Elizabeth Platts. The defendants do not know what relationship Elizabeth was to William Barnes or who William's heir was. Anne has received the rent as guardian to the children from the time of Thomas's death until now. Georges park is held by George Warner rental of £7 10s the rest in the procession of Edward Hadley £5 15s. Edward Hadley said that John Barnes, William's brother did leave Croft Hurst to William Barnes in 1696 and he has paid a yearly rent of £7 10s since

C22/557/27 – Platts V Blaydon 1701 Bridges Division Country Depositions and Affidavits

Interrogatories to be administered to witnesses to be produced, swore and examined on the part on behalf of John Platts and Elizabeth his wife the complainants against Anne Bladon widow, Elizabeth, William, John, Thomas & Mary infants of Anne their mother and guardian and George Warner and Edward Hadley the defendants

1.   Do you know the parties complainants and defendants or any and which of them?

2.   Did you know Henry Bladon of Potter Somersal in the county of Derbyshire yeoman (deceased), Thomas Bladon

of Somersal aforesaid and Elizabeth his wife or any and which of them? Who was the eldest son of the said Thomas and Elizabeth and what relationship was the complainant Elizabeth Platts to the eldest son?

3. Did you know William Barnes the elder of Uttoxeter Woodlands in the county of Stafford (deceased) and was he or any relation to Elizabeth Bladon? What brothers or sisters did William Barnes have what was their names and what became of them? Were any married, who did they marry and what issue did they have?

4. What issue if any did William Barnes the elder have if any? Who did they marry and what issue did they have?

5. Did you know William Barnes the younger of Uttoxeter Woodlands and John Barnes his brother and Ellen their sister? What issue did they have?

6. Do you know of the Manor of Marchington? Is it the same as copyhold manor? Are you aware of heir at law? Have you sat on the jury there and was Elizabeth Platts ever admitted?

7. Did you examine the Parish Register of Somersal Herbert now in the hands of the Minister of Somersal Herbert?

8. What other matter do you know about that may be an advantage to the complainant?

Depositions of witnesses taken at the house of Thomas Lawson in Aston in the county of Derby on the ninth and twentieth day of April in the 13th year of the reign of our Sovereign King William the third before Joseph Hayne, Arthur Bowyer, William Browne and John Barber

Mary, wife of Robert Fletcher of Rocester in the county of Derby, husbandman age three score and four
She knoweth all the parties involved.

She knows Thomas Bladon who was this deponent's grandfather but cannot remember Elizabeth his wife. She heard Elizabeth was the daughter of old William Barnes father of William Barnes the testator; Henry Bladon was the eldest son of the said Thomas Bladon and Elizabeth his wife that the complainant Elizabeth is the daughter of Henry Bladon.

She said William Barnes the elder was brother of Elizabeth Bladon and there were no other brothers, a sister Ellen died unmarried and had no issue. Elizabeth had Henry the eldest son, William, John, Thomas the younger, Mary and Elizabeth. Henry had two daughters Elizabeth the complainant and Dorothy who died without issue.

William Barnes the elder had three children William the testator, John and Ellen all dead without issue

Jane More of Uttoxeter Woodlands in the county of Stafford widow age sixty and one

She knows the parties complainants and defendants.

She knew Henry Bladon and Thomas Bladon she being the granddaughter of the said Thomas Bladon, but never knew Elizabeth the said Thomas Bladon's wife she heard she was the sister to old William Barnes. Henry Bladon was the eldest son of Thomas Bladon by the said Elizabeth and the complainant is the daughter of Henry Bladon.

She knows William Barnes is the brother of Elizabeth Bladon there were no brothers but two sisters the said Elizabeth who married Thomas Bladon and Ellen died unmarried. Thomas had Henry, William, Thomas, John, Mary and Elizabeth. Henry is dead but had Dorothy dead with no issue and Elizabeth the complainant.

William Barnes the elder married and had William, John and Ellen all dead with no issue

James Tomlinson of Loxley in the county of Stafford husbandman age about 70

He knows both the complainants and Anne Bladon, George Warner and Edward Hadley the defendants but not the infant defendants

He knew William Barnes the elder and he had two sisters Elizabeth and Ellen. He knew Ellen well and she died at Uttoxeter unmarried, He believed Elizabeth married Thomas Bladon of Potter Somersal but did not know what issue they had.

William Barnes the elder had two sons William and John and daughter Ellen. He thinks all are dead without issue

Thomas Barber of Marchington Woodlands in the county of Stafford yeoman age 58

He knows both the complainants and Anne Bladon, George Warner and Edward Hadley the defendants but not the infant defendants

He knows Marchington is copyhold manor and he is a copyholder in the Manor. He was on the copyhold jury at a court Baron and court leet about four years ago when Elizabeth was admitted to the copy hold land in the manor to the late estate of William Barnes and Elizabeth was found to be heir at law to William Barnes copyhold land to the estate and admitted tenant there by the steward of the said court. The jury were satisfied with the word.

Thomas Millward of Eaton Dovedale in the county of Derby, gent aged seven and thirty years

He was informed that at the time of the marriage of Thomas Bladon of Potter Somersal in the county of Derby yeoman with Elizabeth Barnes sister to William Barnes the elder of Uttoxeter Woodlands both long since dead. He was shown the parish register of Somersal Herbert and found the entry 22nd October 1604 Thomas Bladon and Elizabeth Barnes married, Thomas Bladon clerk of the church buried 25th March 1697 and Anne Bladon daughter of Anne Bladon widow buried 13th November 1698. The last named Thomas Bladon being husband to the defendant Anne Bladon and Anne buried 1698 was the daughter of Thomas and Anne Bladon the defendant.

Interrogatory to be administered unto witnesses on the part on behalf of the defendants of Anne Bladon widow and others defendants to the bill of complaint of John Platts and his wife complainants

1. Do you know the parties complainants and defendants and how long have you known them? Did you know William Barnes and John Barnes late of Uttoxeter Woodlands in the county of Stafford and Thomas Bladon of Somersal Herbert in the county of Derby and what is his relation to the defendants?

2. Do you know the two pieces of ground called Georges Park and Croft Hurst lying in the parish of Uttoxeter? Was William Barnes the owner?

3. Did the said William Barnes make a will and how long before he died? Who did he intend to give the land Georges Park and Croft Hurst to?

4. Is the paper writing being shown to you the last will and testament of William Barnes did you see him sign seal and publish the will?

5. What did he say as regards the disposal of Georges Park and Croft Hurst?

6. Did you see the deed now being shown to you?

7. Any other matter that may be an advantage to the defendants.

Joan wife of George Bartrum of Uttoxeter Woodlands in the county of Stafford, husbandman age 50 and upwards
She knows the complainants and defendants plus John Barnes, William Barnes and Thomas Bladon. She knows John and William Barnes died about four and a half years ago and Thomas Bladon died about three years ago and the said Thomas was the husband of

Anne Bladon. Elizabeth, John, William, Thomas and Mary are his children.

William Barnes said he would give the closes held by Warner and Hadley to Thomas Bladon and his heirs forever for he had a love for him and for the complainants leave him nothing for if he would he would spend it but for his wife £5

Robert Redfern of Uttoxeter in the county of Stafford husbandman age forty and three and upwards

He knows the defendants and complainants plus John Barnes, William Barnes and Thomas Bladon. William Barnes died in November 1697 and Thomas Bladon Lady Day following. The said Thomas Bladon is the husband of Anne Bladon and father to Elizabeth, William, John, Thomas and Mary.

He knows the land Georges Park and Croft Hurst and that William Barnes was the owner at his death.

When John Barnes lay on his death bed he heard them discussing the two pieces of ground which were jointly seized and they said they would give the grounds to Thomas Bladon for life and then his heirs to share and share alike. If his heirs do not agree for two of them to pay the fine then they might sell the grounds and divide the money. When William Barnes was on his death bed he said the same.

Edward Hadley of Uttoxeter in the county of Stafford grazier aged eight and forty

He holds the ground as he holds Croft Hurst by lease from William Barnes and before that from his brother John Barnes by lease. Since William Barnes death Thomas Bladon was the owner and now Anne Bladon.

He attended the funeral of John Barnes and spoke to William Barnes there who was also very ill and on his deathbed. William said he would give the land to Thomas Bladon a weaver of Somersal Herbert Derbyshire a 'honest, poor man' for his natural life and afterwards to his children along with the land called Georges Park Bramshall.

Thomas Butler of Colton Staffordshire yeoman aged five and thirty

William Barnes made his will about three days before he died and made this deponent one of his executers. William Barnes intended to give the said land to Thomas Bladon for his natural life and then his children to share and share alike. William Barnes said Thomas Bladon was a very honest man. Edward Hadley visited William Barnes the day after he made his will and asked who he had left the said ground to. William Barnes told him Thomas Bladon of Somersal a very honest man.

William Rathbone of Uttoxeter in the county of Stafford gent age five and twenty years

He knew William and John Barnes who are now both dead. He did not know Thomas Bladon but believes William Barnes was a close relation to him and he had a great respect for Thomas Bladon

William Barnes made his will just before his death and this deponent was a witness to the said will. William Barnes did intend to give the said Georges Park and Croft Hurst to Thomas Bladon for his natural life and afterwards to his children. This deponent was sent for and went in great haste to make William Barnes's will who was by then weak in body. His will was made in haste and unfortunately omitted the words of inheritance that should have devised the said Georges Park and Croft Hurst to Thomas Bladon and his heirs forever for that the deponent is deeply sorry but satisfied that that was the wishes of the said William Barnes

C5/328/26 - Platts V Bladen 1703 Derby Bridges Division, four answers

John Platts of Potter Somersal in the county of Derby Yeoman and Elizabeth his wife. Said Anne Bladon widow, Elizabeth, William, John, Thomas and Mary Bladon her children, combined with George Warner, Edward Hadley and Thomas Butler of Colton Stafford gent and William Bladon of Hanbury Stafford clerk. They were seized of the lands Georges Park and Croft Hurst and believed they were entitled to a 6th of the lands as Thomas Bladon had died.

Answers of Thomas Butler one of the defendants to the bill of complaint of John Platts and Elizabeth his wife attaining that William Barnes was seized of the lands in the bill named. William Barnes made his last will and testament in writing bearing the date the four and twenty day of November 1697. He devised to Thomas Bladon of Somersal Herbert in the county of Derby all that close lying near Bramshall Park called Georges Park in the possession of George Warner of Bramshall to Thomas Bladon for his natural life and after his death to be divided amongst his children share and share alike. And the said William Barnes by his will did give and devise to the said Thomas Bladon all that two pieces of land called Croft Hurst in the parish of Uttoxeter in the possession of Edward Hadley for the term of his life and after his death to his children share and share alike. William Barnes gave to the said William Bladon and his heirs forever all the messuage and land in the occupation of George Hunt situated in Uttoxeter to hold for the life of the said William Bladon and his heirs forever. This defendant and William Bladon were appointed executer shortly after publishing his will William Barnes died and the will was proved at Lichfield with the title of the lands and the bond of penalty being £1000 given to William Bladon with the condition that the defendant at any time produce the original will for the title of the lands devised to William Bladon. The defendant has the original will in his procession and he will let the court see it but he does not wish the court to take it off him as he has the greatest share of the estate of William Barnes and should be original will be lost then the title of the estate may be questioned. The original will should not get into the hands of Elizabeth Platts as she is heir at law to William Barnes and entitled to a 6th share of the land devised to Thomas Bladon and his heirs or the value of 40s

C33/302 – Platts V Bladen 8th December 1703 Decrees and order entry books, Michaelmas term

John Platts and Elizabeth his wife (Plaintiffs) complainants Wednesday 8th December and Anne Bladon widow and others defendants counsel on both sides this day attending the right honorable Clerk Nicholas L Keeper Master of the Rolls to be heard touching the matter of the plaintiffs petitions referred to his honor

on 29th November last upon hearing the said petition read and what
was alleged on other side his honor doth order that the said petitions
be dismissed and that the plaintiffs be at liberty to add Thomas
Butler and William Bladon clerk to their bill with appropriate charges
Wednesday 15th December .

C33/304 page 49 – Platts V Bladen 11th December 1704 Decrees and order entry books, Michaelmas term

John Platts and wife Annea querents
Upon a motion this day made unto this court by Mr Banister of
Bladen [missing word] widow Thomas Butler and additional
defendants to the petition in the presence of Mr Jennings "being of
do with the said plaintiffs" [probably some words missing] co-allege that
the plaintiffs shall have an occasion for a commission in this cause
for proving the will of William Barnes which said will the defendant
Butler by his answer to the plaintiff's bill has confessed to have in his
custody, it was therefore prayed that the plaintiff may have a
commission for the proving of the said will and that the defendant
Butler may produce the same at the execution of such commission
and may deliver the same to the plaintiffs upon their giving
reasonable security to redeliver the said will after the hearing of this
cause whereof to the defendants co-insisted that the defendants claim
under the said will and that they ought not to part with the same out
of their custody wherein upon and upon hearing which was alleged
on both sides this court doth order that a commission do issue for
the purpose aforesaid and that the same be executed at such time and
place as the clerk in court on both sides shall agree on And the said
defendant Butler is to send the said will by some person he can trust
therewith to produce the same before the Commission at the
execution of the said commission in order to prove the same and also
at the hearing of this cause

C33/304 page 162 – Platts V Bladen 1704 Decrees and order entry books, Hilary Term

Johom Platt of Eliz and on it querent upon mocon this day made
unto this court by ? Harvey Anna Bladon vid Thom Butler & as
def(endan)ts being of the pl(ain)ti(ff)s co(mpany?) Itt was alleadged yt

[=that] the pl(ain)ti(ffs) have replyed to ye [=the] def(endan)ts answ(er) and served them to reioyne [=rejoin] & forasmuch as this causers only matter of acc(tion)... it was therefore prayed that pub(lishe)d may passe in this clause at the third seale & that the clause may come on to be heard some tyme the next terme which upon producing of an affid(avit?) of notice of this mocon is ordered accordingly

Helena Ruth Bladon Coney

6 VALIDITY OF THE WILL

C22/567/11 – Platts v Butler 25th January 1705 Bridges Division

To be administered to all such witnesses for and on behalf of John & Elizabeth Platts the complainants against Thomas Butler and others the defendants.

1. Do you know the parties complainant or defendant Butler, did you know William Barnes late of Uttoxeter Woodlands and how long since he died?

2. Did you see the paper or parchment now shown unto you purporting to be the last will and testament of William Barnes, signed, sealed and published on 20th November 1697. Did you sign you name as a witness and is it the same signature, did you sign in front of William Barnes?

3. Who had custody of the paper or parchment?

4. What other matter can assist?

Deponents of witnesses taken at the house of Edward Warner in Uttoxeter in the county of Stafford on Thursday the five and twenty day of January 1704 by Arthur Bowyer, John Hayne, William Lathorp and Thomas Sutton on behalf of John Platts and Elizabeth his wife complainants against Thomas Butler and others defendants.

William Lathorp of Uttoxeter in the county of Stafford, aged eight and twenty

He knows John Platts and Thomas Butler but not Elizabeth the wife of John Platts. He was present at the signing of the witnesses to the will. The three witnesses to the said will all signed their names and on being shown the parchment he confirmed all the signatures are genuine

Francis Hunt of Uttoxeter in the county of Stafford, yeoman, aged five and seventy

He knows the complainant John Platts but not Elizabeth his wife, and the defendant Thomas Butler. He was shown the paper and believes it to be the last will and testament of William Barnes and the signatures of William Lathorp, Thomas Webb and himself to be genuine.

Thomas Webb of Woodford in the county of Stafford aged eight and forty

He knows the complainant John Platts and the defendant Thomas Butler but not Elizabeth the wife of John Platts. He did know William Barnes of Uttoxeter Woodlands and he died soon after making his will. He was shown the parchment and believed it to be genuine the last will and testament of William Barnes. The signatures are those of Thomas Webb, Francis Hunt and William Lathorp.

7 AFTERMATH

This is all the paperwork that has been found so far, more may come to light as more Chancery Proceedings are added to the National Archives online catalogue. The result of the Platts v Bladon or Platts v Butler has still to be found but from other evidence it appears that the will was ruled to be genuine and the property distributed as wished by William Barnes.

Thomas Butler

At Lichfield Record Office is a pre-nuptial marriage settlement (D15/11/24/3) dated 1709 between Thomas Butler the younger yeoman of Colton Staffordshire heir apparent of Thomas the elder yeoman and Elizabeth his wife of Burrowsfield Derbyshire and Anne wife of Thomas Butler the younger, sole daughter and heir apparent of John Collier of Colton yeoman of the first part. The second part being William Webb yeoman of Croxall Derbyshire and William Mason yeoman of Donnington Shropshire the 3rd part. The property concerned was Woodgate house in the possession of Anthony Alkins with the ground adjoining in Uttoxeter Moor called Ladies Moor, Pinfold Hurst and Kitchen pieces in the occupation of Thomas Butler; plus farm; messuage and tenement in the parish of Uttoxeter in the occupation of Robert Redfern. The deed states '*The above property and land being devised to the said Thomas Butler and his heirs by William Barnes.'*

John Platts

John died in 1730, after his wife Elizabeth and his will was proved at Lichfield. He makes no mention of any land apart from the lease dated 1689 he holds from George Vernon for a house and farm in Potter Somersal, thought to be the same property that was held for three lives by Thomas Bladon, his son Henry Bladon and Henry's wife Elizabeth. John's niece Hannah Platts (daughter of his brother James) married John Bladon, son of Thomas Bladon of Somersal Herbert in 1716 and one of the infants named in the Georges Park dispute. Thus the two families were now united in marriage.

The Bladon family

No record has been found of Anne's death, although she may have died in 1732 at Uttoxeter as her youngest daughter Mary married there in 1724. Thomas as it states died in 1698 and his estate of £30 16s and 6d was left to Anne his wife. One of the people who drew up his inventory was John Platts.

William Bladon clerk in Holy Orders was Vicar of Hanbury until he died in 1723. Interestingly he wrote in his will '*Last will and testament herby revoking all and all manor of wills therefore by me made either By word or in writing in witness whereof I have ? to this my last will and testament* **Consisting of two sheets of paper** *put my hand and seal this fifteenth day of January anno Domini 1722 in the ninth year of the reign of King George of Great Britain'*
He did own some land at Fauld but this may have come via his wife's family she was a sister of William Browne Vicar of Burton on Trent. His son Isaac Hawkins Browne was a barrister, poet and MP for Much Wenlock Shropshire. William Bladon's son another William was also a Clerk in Holy Orders at Carsington Derbyshire.

Barnes Gift

There was one other bequest William Barnes made known as Barnes gift. This was rental from a messuage and land in Highwoods, then in the possession of John Morris, that William Bladon and his heirs forever were to distribute the annual income (40s or £2) on St

Thomas's Day (21st December) to the poor of Uttoxeter Woodlands. It was thought that those who held the land disposed of the charity and presumably this was as a cash payment at the discretion of the Vestry Committee. This was one of the Bequests taken over by the Uttoxeter Charities Trust in 1860.

Two questions now spring to mind. How much did these cases cost both sides of the family? Unfortunately, the Masters Documents, which includes the accounts, do not survive for any of the suits but you have to wonder how much of the inheritance was spent on the cases, particularly relating to Anne Bladon. She was a widow with a young family to bring up grieving for her husband and then her eldest daughter and was now fighting for her children's rightful inheritance. Thomas left in the region of £2,000 in today's money but I do not suppose that lasted Anne long. The other question I wonder about is what sort of impact this had on the family, split down in middle because of the dispute. My immediate family (Anne and her children) resided a stone's throw from the Platts so must have come across them socially almost daily. As mentioned above, Anne's son John married Hannah Platts, niece of John. The answers to these questions will not be found in the archives and we can only speculate the answer!

Helena Ruth Bladon Coney

	William Barnes died 1654	Ellen Barnes died 1691	John Barnes died 1697	William Barnes died 1697
Woodgate house	Anne Barnes for her life then son William			Thomas Butler
Ladies Moor	Anne Barnes for her life then son William			Thomas Butler
Pinfold Hurst	Anne Barnes for her life then son William			Thomas Butler
Kitchen Piece	Anne Barnes for her life then son William			Thomas Butler
House William do now inhabit	William the younger			
House in Uttoxeter Woodlands Humphrey Biddolph inhabits	John			
Georges Park		John	William	Thomas Bladon

Gorsty Hill house and land				Robert Redfern
Croft Hurst				Thomas Bladon
House and 6 parcels of land inc Newlands where William Barnes now dwells				Thomas Butler
Benjamin Meadow				William Bladon
Marlpitt Ridding				William Bladon
Misty Lane Close, Ditch Botham, Upper & Nether Swansfield and house in possession of George Hunt				William Bladon
House and land in Uttoxeter in possession of John Morris				William Bladon with 40s to poor of Uttoxeter Woodlands

9 KINSHIP REPORT FOR WILLIAM BARNES

This is a list of the main people mentioned in either William Barnes will or were part of the witnesses in the various cases.

Name:	Birth Date:	Relationship:
Abberley, Thomas	1696	Husband of 1st cousin 2x removed
Barnes, Elizabeth		Aunt
Barnes, Ellen		Aunt
Barnes, Ellen	1632	Sister
Barnes, John	1638	Brother
Barnes, William		Father
Billings, Anne		Wife of 1st cousin 1x removed
Bladon, Anne	1679	1st cousin 2x removed
Bladon, Dorothy		1st cousin 1x removed
Bladon, Elizabeth		1st cousin 1x removed
Bladon, Elizabeth	1613	Paternal 1st cousin
Bladon, Elizabeth	06 Oct 1681	1st cousin 2x removed
Bladon, Henry	1604	Paternal 1st cousin
Bladon, John	1610	Paternal 1st cousin
Bladon, John	Bef. 1662	1st cousin 1x removed
Bladon, John	1687	1st cousin 2x removed
Bladon, Margery	1651–1655	1st cousin 1x removed
Bladon, Mary	1606	Paternal 1st cousin
Bladon, Mary	Abt. 1648	1st cousin 1x removed
Bladon, Mary	Abt. 1696	1st cousin 2x removed
Bladon, Thomas	1577	Husband of aunt
Bladon, Thomas	Aft. 1610	Paternal 1st cousin
Bladon, Thomas	1646	1st cousin 1x removed
Bladon, Thomas	1687	1st cousin 2x removed
Bladon, Thomas	1694	1st cousin 2x removed
Bladon, William	1608	Paternal 1st cousin
Bladon, William	Bef. 1654	1st cousin 1x removed
Bladon, William	1662	1st cousin 1x removed
Bladon, William	1683	1st cousin 2x removed
Botham, William		Husband of 1st cousin 1x removed
Browne, Elizabeth	1669	Wife of 1st cousin 1x removed
Coates, Francis	1648	Husband of 1st cousin 1x removed
Dilks, Elias	1645	Husband of 1st cousin 1x removed
Fletcher, Robert		Husband of 1st cousin 1x removed
Hinton, Rebecca	1649	Wife of 1st cousin 1x removed
Moore, Richard		Husband of 1st cousin 1x removed

Oldfield, Edward	1636	1st cousin 1x removed
Oldfield, Humphrey	1648	1st cousin 1x removed
Oldfield, Jane	1640	1st cousin 1x removed
Oldfield, Joane	1645	1st cousin 1x removed
Oldfield, Mary	1639	1st cousin 1x removed
Oldfield, Richard	1605	Husband of 1st cousin
Oldfield, Richard	1634	1st cousin 1x removed
Oldfield, William	1637	1st cousin 1x removed
Platts, John	Abt. 1657	Husband of 1st cousin 1x removed
Stottwell, Anne		Mother

Genealogical Chart

First Generation

1. **Unknown BARNES** has few details recorded about him.

   Unknown BARNES had the following children:

+2	William BARNES (-1654)
+3	Ellen BARNES (-1650)
+4	Elizabeth BARNES (-bef1641)

Second Generation

2. **William BARNES**, son of Unknown BARNES, died in 1654 in Uttoxeter Woodlands Staffordshire. He was buried on 4 July 1654 in Uttoxeter, Staffordshire. He married **ANN Stottwell**.

   ANN Stottwell died in Uttoxeter Woodlands Staffordshire and was buried on 11 March 1668 in Uttoxeter Staffordshire. She and William BARNES had the following children:

+5	Ellen BARNES (1632-1691)
+6	William BARNES (1634-1697)
+7	John BARNES (1638-1697)

3. **Ellen BARNES**, daughter of Unknown BARNES, was buried on 3 October 1650 in Uttoxeter Staffordshire.

4. **Elizabeth BARNES**, daughter of Unknown BARNES, married **Thomas BLADON** on 22 November 1604 in Somersal Herbert, Derbyshire. She died between 1613 and 1641 in Potter Somersal, Derbyshire.

Thomas BLADON was baptised on 29 April 1577 in Findern Derbyshire. He was a Husbandman and died circa 1655 in Potter Somersal Derbyshire.

on 7th July 1641, Thomas and his son Henry were issued with a lease by *Sir Edward Vernon of Sudbury knight and Dame Margaret his wife to Thomas Bladon of Potter Somersal husbandman and Henry his son and Elizabeth, Henrys wife in consideration of £60 and all their messuage, farm or tenement with all barns etc in Potter Somersal now in Thomas's occupation to hold for 3 lives at £4 per annum.*

Thomas BLADON and Elizabeth BARNES had the following children:

> +8   Henry BLADON (1604-1676)
>
> +9   Mary BLADON (1606-1667)
>
> +10   William BLADON (1608-1669)
>
> +11   John BLADON (1610-1686)
>
> +12   Thomas BLADON (aft1610-1680)
>
> +13   Elizabeth BLADON (1613-bef1650)

Third Generation

5. **Ellen BARNES**, daughter of William BARNES and ANN Stottwell, was baptised on 8 July 1632 in Uttoxeter, Staffordshire. She was buried on 10 November 1691 in Uttoxeter Staffordshire.

6. **William BARNES**, son of William BARNES and ANN Stottwell, was baptised on 5 February 1634 in Uttoxeter Staffordshire. He died on 23 November 1697 in Uttoxeter Woodlands Staffordshire and was buried on 29 November 1697 in Uttoxeter Staffordshire. William was a yeoman.

7. **John BARNES**, son of William BARNES and ANN Stottwell, was baptised on 1 January 1638 in Uttoxeter Staffordshire. He was buried on 25 November 1697 in Uttoxeter Staffordshire and was also a yeoman.

8. **Henry BLADON**, son of Thomas BLADON and Elizabeth BARNES, was born in 1604 in Potter Somersal, Derbyshire and baptised in Somersal Herbert, Derbyshire. He was a Yeoman and married **Elizabeth** before 1641. He died in Potter Somersal Derbyshire and was buried on 1 March 1676 in Sudbury, Derbyshire.

Henry rented a farm and land from Sir Edward Vernon along with his father for 3 lives - lease for life at £4 per year consisting of 35 1/2 acres.
He left £113 to daughter Dorothy, and the rest of his estate to wife Elizabeth £241 8s He received £10 in aunt Ellen Barnes will

Elizabeth died in 1685 in Potter Somersal Derbyshire and was buried on 2 January 1685 in Sudbury Derbyshire. She continued to resided at the farm rented from the Vernon's being the 3rd life After her death John Platts and his wife took over

Elizabeth and Henry BLADON had the following children:

+14   Elizabeth BLADON (-1721)

+15   Dorothy BLADON (-1696)

9. **Mary BLADON**, daughter of Thomas BLADON and Elizabeth BARNES, was born in 1606 in Potter Somersal Derbyshire and baptised on 22 October 1606 in Somersal Herbert Derbyshire. She married **Richard OLDFIELD** on 10 November

1631 in Uttoxeter Staffordshire. She died in 1667 in Blounts Uttoxeter Staffordshire and was buried on 29 May 1667 in Uttoxeter Staffordshire.

Mary left a will and son Edward was to look after Humphrey, sons Richard, William and Edward received 1s, daughter Mary £7 and Jane £4.

Richard OLDFIELD was baptised on 1 June 1605 in Uttoxeter Staffordshire. He was buried on 30 September 1655 in Uttoxeter Staffordshire. He and Mary BLADON had the following children:

> +16   Edward OLDFIELD (1632-1634)
>
> +17   Richard OLDFIELD (1634-aft1691)
>
> +18   Edward OLDFIELD (1636-1718)
>
> +19   William OLDFIELD (1637-1691)
>
> +20   Mary OLDFIELD (1639-1713)
>
> +21   Jane OLDFIELD (1640-aft1701)
>
> +22   Joane OLDFIELD (1645-1645)
>
> +23   Humphrey OLDFIELD (1648-1671)

10. **William BLADON**, son of Thomas BLADON and Elizabeth BARNES, was born in 1608 in Potter Somersal Derbyshire and baptised on 22 February 1608 in Somersal Herbert Derbyshire. He married **Judith** before 1646 and secondly married **Bridget ELLIOT** on 24 September 1657 in Somersal Herbert Derbyshire. He was buried on 2 February 1669 in Somersal Herbert Derbyshire.

He received £10 in aunt Ellen Barnes will.

Judith was buried on 28 December 1656 in Somersal Herbert Derbyshire. She and William BLADON had the following children:

+24   Thomas BLADON (1646-1698)

+25   William BLADON (bef 1654-1712)

+26   John BLADON (1655-1655)

+27   Hannah BLADON (1656-1656)

Bridget ELLIOT was buried on 26 January 1683 in Somersal Herbert Derbyshire.

Bridget left a will and bequeathed to her God daughter Mary Noon of Sudbury Derbyshire £9, her coffer and clothes to Thomas Bladon plus £5, Rev Edward Shand of Somersal Herbert £1, Cousin Thomas Elliott 1s, James Elliott 1s, Margery Bladon 10s, Cousin Charles Bickleys children 10s each, William Gallimore 1s to buy gloves and William Bladon 1s to buy gloves,

11. **John BLADON**, son of Thomas BLADON and Elizabeth BARNES, was born in 1610 in Potter Somersal Derbyshire. He was baptised on 26 December 1610 in Somersal Herbert Derbyshire and was a Yeoman. He married **Elizabeth YEOMAN** on 1 June 1643 in Doveridge, Derbyshire. He died in 1686 in West Broughton Derbyshire and was buried on 10 January 1686 in Doveridge Derbyshire.

John rented a messuage or tenement in West Broughton from John Fitzherbert of Somersal Herbert Esq. for £340 with Barns, gardens, croft and pasture. 3acres close of meadow, little cans 1 acres, 5 acres meadow in Broughton eyes, 2 acres in Broad Meadow, clike 3 acres, New gate 2 acres, gorsy close 9 acres. from 1659 for £12 per year and 8 acres in Hill Somersal
He left son John all tenements and land in West Broughton which he purchased from John Fitzherbert, son William 1s his daughters £40 each, daughter Mary Botham £12 his total estate was £120 13s 8d. He also received £10 in aunt Ellen Barnes will

Elizabeth YEOMAN was buried on 27 January 1712 in Doveridge Derbyshire. She and John BLADON had the following children:

+28   Mary BLADON (c. 1648-aft1702)

+29   Margery BLADON (aft1651-1727)

+30   John BLADON (bef1662-1733)

+31   William BLADON (1662-1723)

12. **Thomas BLADON**, son of Thomas BLADON and Elizabeth BARNES, was born after 1610 in Potter Somersal Derbyshire. He was buried on 9 October 1680 in Sudbury Derbyshire.

He received £10 in aunt Ellen Barnes will.

13. **Elizabeth BLADON**, daughter of Thomas BLADON and Elizabeth BARNES, was born in 1613 in Potter Somersal Derbyshire. She was baptised on 25 April 1613 in Somersal Herbert Derbyshire and died before 1650.

Fourth Generation

14. **Elizabeth BLADON**, daughter of Henry BLADON and Elizabeth, was born in Potter Somersal, Derbyshire. She married **John PLATTS** on 30 October 1676 in Sudbury, Derbyshire. She died in 1721 in Potter Somersal Derbyshire and was buried on 15 February 1721 in Sudbury Derbyshire.

She received £5 in the will of William Barnes her father's cousin.

John PLATTS was born circa 1657 and was a Yeoman. He died in 1729 in Potter Somersal Derbyshire and was buried on 26 December 1729 in Sudbury Derbyshire.

In his will he bequeathed the lease of his house and farm at Potter Somersal to his son John but he was to pay 10s per year to his daughter Hannah Roome, his son in law John Roome 1s, his 3 grandsons John, Thomas and James Platts bed, cupboard, 5 pewter dishes, 12 pewter plates and one brass rootle, pewter tankard, 2 brass pans, coffer, long table and brass pot. His cow and mare to son his John.

15. **Dorothy BLADON**, daughter of Henry BLADON and Elizabeth, was born in Potter Somersal Derbyshire. She married **Francis COATES** on 11 June 1677 in Sudbury Derbyshire. She was buried on 28 May 1696 in Sudbury Derbyshire.

She received £113 in her father's will.

Francis COATES was baptised on 25 July 1648 in Leigh Staffordshire. He was a Yeoman. He died in 1683 in Withington Staffordshire and was buried on 29 December 1683 in Leigh Staffordshire.

16. **Edward OLDFIELD**, son of Richard OLDFIELD and Mary BLADON, was baptised on 1 October 1632 in Uttoxeter Staffordshire and buried there on 30 May 1634.

17. **Richard OLDFIELD**, son of Richard OLDFIELD and Mary BLADON, was baptised on 14 September 1634 in Uttoxeter Staffordshire. He was a Skinner and died after 1691.

He received 1s in his mothers will, £5 in his grandfather Edward Oldfields will and the household goods in his great aunt Ellen Barnes will.

18. **Edward OLDFIELD**, son of Richard OLDFIELD and Mary BLADON, was baptised on 3 April 1636 in Uttoxeter Staffordshire. He was a postmaster and buried on 17 July 1718 in Uttoxeter Staffordshire. He married **MARY**.

He was asked to maintain his brother Humphrey by his mother, received £10 in his grandfather Edward Oldfields will, received £5 in the will of William Barnes his mothers cousin, received £20 in the will of great aunt Ellen Barnes. and left £31 to his daughter Jane

19. **William OLDFIELD**, son of Richard OLDFIELD and Mary BLADON, was baptised on 15 October 1637 in Uttoxeter Staffordshire. He married **Rebecca HINTON** on 9 December 1668 in St Mary Stafford Staffordshire. He was buried on 28 June 1691 in Uttoxeter Staffordshire.

He received 1s in his mothers will and £20 in the will of great aunt Ellen Barnes.

Rebecca HINTON was baptised on 16 June 1649 in Hanbury Staffordshire. She died after 1697.
Received £5 in the will of William Barnes.

20. **Mary OLDFIELD**, daughter of Richard OLDFIELD and Mary BLADON, was baptised on 27 August 1639 in Uttoxeter Staffordshire. She married **Robert FLETCHER** after 1667 and was buried on 7 February 1713 in Rocester Staffordshire.

She received £7 in her mother's will and £5 in her grandfather Edward Oldfields will and £20 in the will of great aunt Ellen Barnes.

Robert FLETCHER was baptised on 15 April 1643 in Rocester Staffordshire and was buried on 8 December 1709 in Rocester Staffordshire.

21. **Jane OLDFIELD**, daughter of Richard OLDFIELD and Mary BLADON, was baptised on 25 February 1640 in Uttoxeter Staffordshire. She married **Richard MOORE** after 1667 and died after 1701 in Uttoxeter Woodlands Staffordshire.

Received £4 in her mother's will and £20 in the will of great aunt Ellen Barnes and some of her household effects.

Richard MOORE died between 1688 and 1701 in Uttoxeter Woodlands Staffordshire.

22. **Joane OLDFIELD**, daughter of Richard OLDFIELD and Mary BLADON, was baptised on 2 November 1645 in Uttoxeter . Staffordshire. She was buried on 11 November 1645 in Uttoxeter Staffordshire

23. **Humphrey OLDFIELD**, son of Richard OLDFIELD and Mary BLADON, was baptised on 13 August 1648 in Uttoxeter Staffordshire . He was buried on 12 April 1671 in Uttoxeter Staffordshire.

24. **Thomas BLADON**, son of William BLADON and Judith, was baptised on 4 March 1646 in Doveridge Derbyshire. He was a Webster and Weaver. He married **Anne BILLINGS** on 1 May 1679 in Somersal Herbert, Derbyshire. He was buried on 25 March 1698 in Somersal Herbert Derbyshire.

He received 1s in his step mothers will to buy gloves and left £30 16s 6d to wife Anne when he died In the will of William Barnes, his father's cousin he received all that close lying near Bramshall Park called Georges Parks in the possession of George Warner of Bramshall, for the natural life of Thomas and after his death to be divided between Thomas's children after his death. Two pieces with barn standing on them called Croft Hurst in Uttoxeter in the possession of Edward Hadley. To be divided between Thomas's children after the death of Thomas Bladon his death.

Anne BILLINGS was possibly born in Cubley Derbyshire and died was buried on 24 January 1732 in Uttoxeter Staffordshire.

She received 2s 6d from her brother in law William to buy a pair of gloves in his will

Anne BILLINGS and Thomas BLADON had the following children:

+32 Anne BLADON (1679-1698)

+33 Elizabeth BLADON (1681-aft1754)

+34 William BLADON (1683-1754)

+35 John BLADON (1687-1728)

+36 Thomas BLADON (1687-1687)

+37   Thomas BLADON (1694-1732)

+38   Mary BLADON (c. 1696-1768)

25. **William BLADON**, son of William BLADON and Judith, was born before 1654 and was a Husbandman. He married **Alice RUSDEN** on 8 May 1679 in Stretton-En-Le-Fields Leicestershire. He died on 14 March 1712 in Stretten-En-Le-Fields Leicestershire.

He received 1s in his step mothers will to buy gloves and left Anne 2s 6d to buy pair of gloves, his nephews 4s each and nieces 10s rest to his wife.

Alice RUSDEN died in 1733 in Stretten-En-Le-Fields Leicestershire.

She left to each of her Bladon nephews and nieces £5.

26. **John BLADON**, son of William BLADON and Judith, was born in 1655 and buried on 16 March 1655 in Somersal Herbert Derbyshire.

27. **Hannah BLADON**, daughter of William BLADON and Judith, was born and baptised on 20 November 1656 in Somersal Herbert Derbyshire. She was buried on 27 December 1656 in Somersal Herbert Derbyshire.

28. **Mary BLADON**, daughter of John BLADON and Elizabeth YEOMAN, was born circa 1648 in Derbyshire. She married **William BOTHAM** on 6 July 1668 in Somersal Herbert Derbyshire. She died after 1702.

She received £12 in her father's will and received £5 in the will of William Barnes her father's cousin.

William BOTHAM died in 1688 in Roston, Derbyshire. He was buried on 14 April 1688 in Norbury, Derbyshire.

He left £138 18s 8d.

29. **Margery BLADON**, daughter of John BLADON and Elizabeth YEOMAN, was born between 1651 and 1655 in Derbyshire. She married **Elias DILKS** in 1695 at Marston on Dove or St Werburgh Derby Derbyshire. She died in 1727 in Hatton, Derbyshire and was buried on 18 February 1727 in Marston on Dove, Derbyshire.

She received 10s in the will of Bridget Bladon, £40 in her father's will and £5 in the will of William Barnes her father's cousin

Elias DILKS was baptised on 29 May 1645 in Church Broughton Derbyshire. He died in 1728 in Hatton Derbyshire and was buried on 13 September 1728 in Marston on Dove Derbyshire.

30. **John BLADON**, son of John BLADON and Elizabeth YEOMAN, was born before 1662 in Derbyshire and was a Yeoman. He married **Mary COTTON** in 1691 in Marchington Staffordshire. He died in 1733 in West Broughton Derbyshire and was buried on 23 January 1733 in Doveridge Derbyshire.

He received all the land and tenements in West Broughton in his father's will and £5 in the will of William Barnes his father's cousin

31. **William BLADON**, son of John BLADON and Elizabeth YEOMAN, was born in 1662 in Derbyshire. He was educated at Trinity College Cambridge between 1678 and 1682. On 29 May 1686 he was an Ordained by Bishop Henry Compton in London and became Rector of Somersal Herbert Derbyshire. He married **Elizabeth BROWNE** on 31 July 1688 in Somersal Herbert. In 1690 he became Vicar of Hanbury Staffordshire. He died in 1723 in Fauld Staffordshire and was buried on 20 February 1723 in Hanbury Staffordshire.

He received 1s in his father's will and 1 guinea in his mother in laws will. He left his wife his silver tankard, tables, bed linen, bed in the best chamber, bed in the red chamber, 4 pewter dishes, 12 pewter plates, 1 table and 5 chairs. Son William £60, brewing copper, books and manuscripts, daughter Mary £150 and chest of drawers in the best chamber, son John £105, daughter Elizabeth £25, son James £25 and daughter Jane £25. In the will of William Barnes his father's cousin he received all the herding and quick stock which belong to me. The messague and land in the parish of Uttoxeter, now in possession of George Hunt to William Bladon and his heirs forever. Two closes called Benjamin Meadow and Marlpitt Ridding in Marchington Woodlands with the said appurtenances to him and his heirs forever. A messague and croft in the parish of Uttoxeter in possession of John Morris to William and his heirs forever paying the sum of 40s per year to the poor of Uttoxeter Woodlands forever

Elizabeth BROWNE was born in Woodford Staffordshire and baptised on 24 March 1669 in Uttoxeter Staffordshire. She died in Fauld Staffordshire and buried on 5 September 1728 in Hanbury Staffordshire inside the church.

She received a guinea in her cousin John Challoners will and a guinea in her mother's will.

Fifth Generation

32. **Anne BLADON**, daughter of Thomas BLADON and Anne BILLINGS, was baptised on 4 March 1679 in Somersal Herbert Derbyshire. She died on 9 November 1698 in Somersal Herbert Derbyshire and buried on 13 November 1698 in Somersal Herbert Derbyshire.

In the will of William Barnes, her grandfathers cousin she received two feather beds in the house where William Barnes now dwells, one where the serving maids lie and the other in the chamber over the house.

33. **Elizabeth BLADON**, daughter of Thomas BLADON and Anne BILLINGS, was baptised on 6 October 1681 in Somersal Herbert Derbyshire. She died after 1754 and married **John WOOLLEY**.

She received 10s in her uncle's will, £5 in her aunts will and £10 in her brothers will

In the will of William Barnes, her grandfathers cousin she

received two feather beds in the house where William Barnes now dwells, one where the serving maids lie and the other in the chamber over the house.

34. **William BLADON**, son of Thomas BLADON and Anne BILLINGS, was baptised on 6 March 1683 in Somersal Herbert Derbyshire. He was a Yeoman and married **Ann HARRISON** on 11 July 1708 in Hanbury, Staffordshire. He died in 1754 in Hill Somersal, Derbyshire being buried on 1 September 1754 in Sudbury, Derbyshire.

He received 4s in his uncles will and £5 in his aunts will His will made in 1754 states Nephew Thomas Bladon residing with him household goods, implements, bedding, woollen, pewter, brass, wearing apparel, husbandry wear, all other goods. (son of brother John Bladon) also executer. Godson John Harrison £10 and executer, William Harrison yeoman of Hill Somersal £10, Ann Hayne daughter of John Harrison of Hill Somersal £10 yeoman, and chest belonging to late wife, Elizabeth Wood of Ellaston £10, Ann Wood £5. Thomas Abberley the younger, William Abberley, Ann Abberley, Catherine Abberley children of Thomas Abberley the elder and Mary of Newton, parish of Blithfield £20 between them. Sister Elizabeth Woolley £10, John Woolley son of Elizabeth £5, Thomas Bladon of Marston Montgomery and sisters Dorothy and Ellen Bladon £20 between them, Elizabeth Tomlinson of Duffield widow £10. Total estate £120 10s. The witness were John Bladon senior and John Bladon junior.

Ann HARRISON was baptised on 21 June 1688 in Sudbury Derbyshire. She died in 1743 in Hill Somersal Derbyshire and was buried on 23 April 1743 in Sudbury Derbyshire.

35. **John BLADON**, son of Thomas BLADON and Anne BILLINGS, was baptised on 22 January 1687 in Somersal Herbert Derbyshire. He was a Webster and Weaver and married **Hannah PLATTS** on 10 May 1716 in Doveridge, Derbyshire. He was buried on 13 February 1728 in Doveridge Derbyshire

He received 4s in his uncles will and £5 in his aunts will

Hannah PLATTS was born in 1692 in Hill Somersal. She was baptised on 15 May 1692 in Sudbury Derbyshire. She died in 1728 in St Alkmond Derby Derbyshire and was buried on 19 February 1728 in Doveridge Derbyshire. She was a niece of John Platts who married Elizabeth Bladon

36. **Thomas BLADON**, son of Thomas BLADON and Anne BILLINGS, was born in 1687 in Somersal Herbert Derbyshire. He was buried on 10 February 1687 in Somersal Herbert Derbyshire.

37. **Thomas BLADON**, son of Thomas BLADON and Anne BILLINGS, was baptised on 18 October 1694 in Somersal Herbert Derbyshire. He married **Hannah MELLOR** on 31 December 1719 in St Margaret Wetton Staffordshire. His second wife was **Dorothy HARVEY** who he married on 3 January 1722 in Checkley Staffordshire. He died in 1732 in Hill Somersal Derbyshire and was buried on 7 March 1732 in Sudbury Derbyshire.

He received 4s in his uncles will, £5 in his aunts will

Hannah MELLOR died in 1721 in Wetton Staffordshire and was buried on 12 September 1721 in St Margaret Wetton Staffordshire.

Dorothy HARVEY was baptised on 26 October 1694 in Checkley Staffordshire. She was buried on 16 November 1741 in Sudbury Derbyshire.

38. **Mary BLADON**, daughter of Thomas BLADON and Anne BILLINGS, was born circa 1696 in Somersal Herbert Derbyshire. She married **Thomas ABBERLEY** on 11 June 1724 in Uttoxeter, Staffordshire. She died in 1768 in Blithfield Staffordshire and was buried on 26 February 1768 in Blithfield Staffordshire.

She received 10s in her uncle's will and £5 in her aunts will.

Thomas ABBERLEY was born in 1696 and was a Husbandman. He died in 1771 in Newton Staffordshire and was buried on 19 March 1771 in Blithfield Staffordshire.

He left his estate to Son Thomas of Hollington £5, son Walter Oak Meadow lying in Abbotts Bromley, chest, son William £80, daughter Ann £40, daughter Catherine North wife of John of Osgathorpe 1s, daughters Mary and Margaret £60 and son John rest of the estate.

ABOUT THE AUTHOR

Helena Coney became interested in family history at the age of 15. After spending 2 years researching her maternal grandmothers maiden name she decided to research her own name of Bladon. Some 26 years later research is back to the late 1400's to the area where she now resides! She has written a book on her own Bladon family and is researching Bladon's all over the world Her web site is https://sites.google.com/site/bladonfamilyhistory/